Seasons

Teresa Heapy

Houghton Mifflin Harcourt.

Seasons was originally published in English in 2016. This edition is published by arrangement with Oxford University Press.

U.S. Edition copyright © 2019 by Houghton Mifflin Harcourt Publishing Company
Text and illustrations © Oxford University Press 2016

Printed in China

ISBN 978-0-358-26164-3

1 2 3 4 5 6 7 8 9 10   XXXX   28 27 26 25 24 23 22 21 20 19

4500000000   A B C D E F G

Concept © Teresa Heapy 2016
Illustrations © Kristyna Litten 2016
Inside cover notes written by Teresa Heapy

Acknowledgments

Series Editor: Nikki Gamble

The publisher would like to thank the following for permission to reproduce photographs:
Cover and **p9tl:** Rebell/Shutterstock; **p1&p11bl:** GrahamMoore999/ Shutterstock; **p5tl:** Nicky Rhodes/Shutterstock; **p5tr&5br:** Life on White/ Bigstock; **p5bl:** Alasdair Thomson/istock; **p7tl:** Tierfotoagentur/Alamy Stock Photo; **p7tr:** blickwinkel/Alamy Stock Photo; **p7bl:** Mode Images/ Alamy Stock Photo; **p7br:** eyasspics/Alamy Stock Photo; **p9tr:** nelea33/ Shutterstock; **p9bl:** Korvit/Bigstock; **p9br:** Alyce Taylor/Alamy Stock Photo; **p11tl:** Roberto Zocchi/istock; **p11tr:** Andrea Casali/Alamy Stock Photo; **p11br:** Ian Grainger/Shutterstock.

Houghton Mifflin Harcourt Publishing Company
125 High Street
Boston, MA 02110
www.hmhco.com

Cover (sticker) © Alexander Lysenko/Shutterstock
p. 4, p. 8, p. 12 © Petr Vaclavek/Shutterstock

Contents

It is spring.

It is summer.

It is fall.

HMH

Nonfiction text features such as diagrams, picture glossaries, and tables of contents are introduced to early learners.

It is winter.

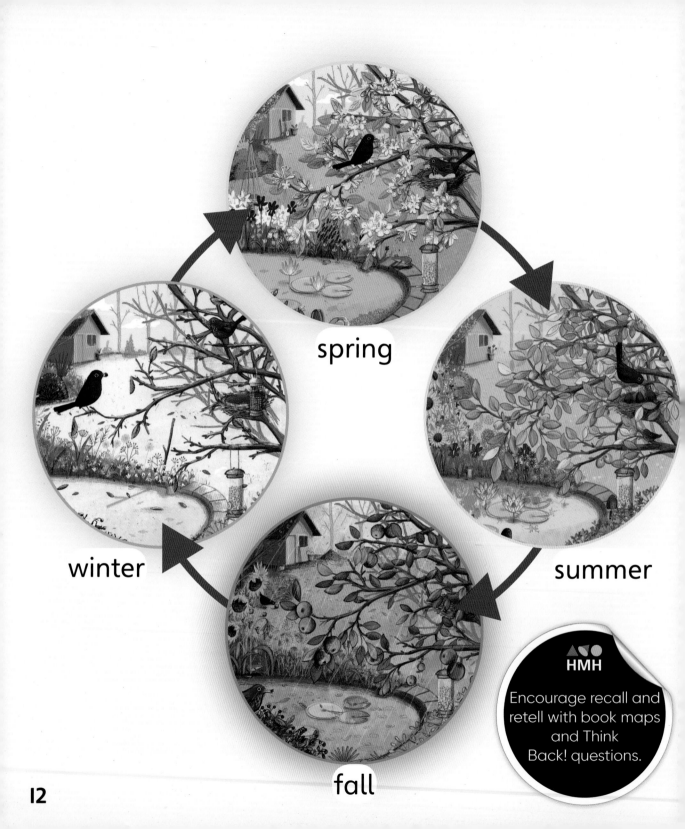

spring

summer

fall

winter

GLOSSARY

extinct (ek-STINGKT): Having no living members

fossils (FOSS-uhlz): Remains or traces of plants or animals from millions of years ago

herbivore (UR-buh-vor): An animal that eats only plants

paleontologists (pay-lee-uhn-TOL-uh-jists): Scientists who study fossils

predators (PRED-uh-turz): Animals that hunt other animals for food

prey (PRAY): Animals hunted and eaten by other animals

sauropod (SOR-uh-pahd): Any type of dinosaur that belonged to the group with long necks, small heads, that walked on four feet, and ate only plants

serrated (SER-ay-tid): Having a jagged, saw-like edge

theropods (THER-uh-pahdz): Dinosaurs that walked and ran on two feet, had three toes on each foot, and most had sharp teeth and claws

INDEX

School-to-Home Support for Caregivers and Teachers

This book helps children grow by letting them practice reading. Here are a few guiding questions to help the reader build his or her comprehension skills. Possible answers appear here in red.

Before Reading

- **What do I think this book is about?** *I think this book is about giant dinosaurs that looked creepy. I think this book is about cool dinosaurs.*

- **What do I want to learn about this topic?** *I want to learn what happened to the dinosaurs. I want to learn what dinosaurs ate and where they lived.*

During Reading

- **I wonder why...** *I wonder why some dinosaurs ate meat while others only ate plants. I wonder why dinosaurs were so large.*

- **What have I learned so far?** *I have learned that humans never lived on Earth at the same time as dinosaurs. I have learned that Tyrannosaurus Rex could run up to 33 mph (53 kph).*

After Reading

- **What details did I learn about this topic?** *I have learned that scientists learn more about dinosaurs by studying their bones, footprints, teeth, and poop. They can tell what kind of food dinosaurs ate by studying their poop.*

- **Read the book again and look for the glossary words.** *I see the word* ***paleontologists*** *on page 20 and the word* ***extinct*** *on page 22. The other glossary words are found on page 23.*

Library and Archives Canada Cataloguing in Publication

Title: Dinosaurs / Alan Walker.
Names: Walker, Alan, 1963- author.
Description: Series statement: Creepy but cool | "A Crabtree seedlings book". | Includes index. | Previously published in electronic format by Blue Door Education in 2020.
Identifiers: Canadiana (print) 20210201789 | Canadiana (ebook) 20210201797 | ISBN 9781427161659 (hardcover) | ISBN 9781427161772 (softcover) | ISBN 9781427161895 (HTML) | ISBN 9781427162014 (EPUB) | ISBN 9781427162137 (read-along ebook)
Subjects: LCSH: Dinosaurs—Juvenile literature.
Classification: LCC QE861.5 .W335 2022 | DDC j567.9—dc23

Library of Congress Cataloging-in-Publication Data

Names: Walker, Alan, 1963- author.
Title: Dinosaurs / Alan Walker.
Description: New York : Crabtree Publishing, [2022] | Series: Creepy but cool - a Crabtree seedlings book | Includes index.
Identifiers: LCCN 2021018435 (print) | LCCN 2021018436 (ebook) | ISBN 9781427161659 (hardcover) | ISBN 9781427161772 (paperback) | ISBN 9781427161895 (ebook) | ISBN 9781427162014 (epub) | ISBN 9781427162137
Subjects: LCSH: Dinosaurs--Juvenile literature.
Classification: LCC QE861.5 .W325 2022 (print) | LCC QE861.5 (ebook) DDC 567.9--dc23
LC record available at https://lccn.loc.gov/2021018435
LC ebook record available at https://lccn.loc.gov/2021018436

Crabtree Publishing Company

www.crabtreebooks.com   1–800–387–7650

Print book version produced jointly with Blue Door Education in 2022

Written by Alan Walker

Print coordinator: Katherine Berti

Printed in the U.S.A./062021/CG20210401

Published in the United States
Crabtree Publishing
347 Fifth Ave.
Suite 1402-145
New York, NY 10016

Published in Canada
Crabtree Publishing
616 Welland Ave.
St. Catharines, Ontario
L2M 5V6